African-American Inventions That Changed The World

Influential Inventors and Their Revolutionary Creations

Michael A. Carson

Copyright © 2017 by Michael A. Carson

Double Infinity Publishing
P. O. Box 55 Grayson, GA 30017

Printed in the United States of America

African-American Inventions That Change The World

Contributing Editor: Shenika H. Carson
Cover Design: Double Infinity Publishing
Design Director: Shenika H. Carson

ISBN-13: 978-0692949399
ISBN-10: 0692949399

Double Infinity Publishing books may be purchased
in bulk at a special discount for sales promotion, corporate
gifts, fund-raising or educational purposes. For details, contact
the Special Sales Department, Double Infinity Publishing,
P.O. Box 55 Grayson, GA. 30017 or by email at
DoubleInfinityPublishing1@Gmail.com.

DEDICATION

This book is dedicated to the love of my life, my beautiful wife Shenika, thank you for all of your love and support. To my son Matthew, who inspired me to write this book, I love you and I am very proud of you.

To the thousands of African-American men and women inventors who were not allowed to receive a U.S. Patent for their inventions prior to the early 1800's. While your names were never mentioned in history books, your contributions to the world will never be forgotten.

To the next generation of African-American innovators who continue to thrive, push the limits and challenge themselves to create new ideas and write the next chapter in world history.

Other Publications By Author: Michael A. Carson

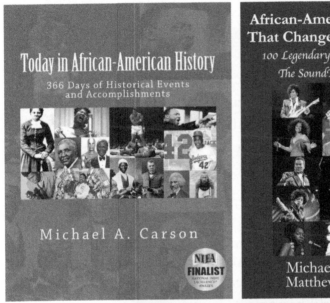

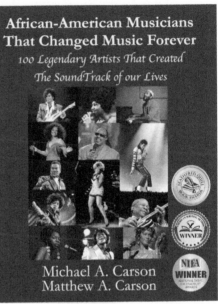

"Education is the key to unlock the golden door of freedom"

"When you do the common things in life in an uncommon way, you will command the attention of the world"

"Ninety-nine percent of failures come from people who have a habit of making excuses"

"Where there is no Vision, there is no Hope"

George Washington Carver...

"The color of the skin is no way connected with strength of the mind or intellectual powers"

Benjamin Banneker...

"If I have accomplished anything in life it is because I have been willing to work hard"

Madam C.J. Walker...

"We create our future, by well improving present opportunities, however few and small they be"

Lewis Latimer...

"Change will not come if we wait for some other person or some other time. We are the ones we've been waiting for. We are the change we seek"

President Barack Obama...

Double Infinity Publishing

CONTENTS

Introduction

A considerable amount of the world's most influential inventors have been African-American, which is a fact that is often overlooked.

Throughout history, African-Americans inventors have played a pivotal role in creating revolutionary inventions that have impacted our lives in various ways. These pioneers have contributed to the fields of medicine, agriculture, science and technology, to name a few.

In the 1800's, many of these innovators were born into slavery and were not allowed to acquire a formal education, they were faced with countless obstacles and had to triumph over many adverse conditions. Nevertheless, these inventors have made significant contributions to the world.

African-American men and women have left their mark in both American and World History. Many of their innovative creations would not exist today if it wasn't for their brilliant minds and creative ideas.

The incredible inventors mentioned in this book have collectively created over 500 inventions. They represent some of the amazing men and women who have impacted our lives through their intelligence and ingenuity.

George Washington Carver

Inventions:

George Washington Carver was an Artist, College Educator, Chemist, Botanist and the man who raised the peanut and soybean to cash crops that helped save the South's farming economy. He issued bulletins to farmers explaining how growing peanuts instead of cotton was better for the nutrients in the soil. He also developed hundreds of uses from peanuts including soap, axle grease, insecticides, glue, medicines and charcoal to name a few. Contrary to popular belief, he did not invent peanut butter. For all his research and accomplishments, Carver only patented three of his peanut inventions, he was not interested in fame or fortune. All of what he was able to produce from peanuts led to it becoming one of the six most produced crops in the U.S. by the 1940's. Carver revolutionized agriculture in the South, transforming its economy. The United States Postal Service honored Carver on the Postage Stamp in 1948 and 1998. He was also inducted into the National Inventors Hall of Fame in 1990.

George Washington Carver

(1864 – 1943)

Background: George Washington Carver's birthdate is unknown, he was born in Diamond Grove, Missouri in 1864 to enslaved parents. He was orphaned as an infant and raised by the owners of a plantation. Growing up he discovered his love of plants and nature, he was determined to pursue an education to learn more about them. Carver was later adopted by foster parents, they allowed him to attend school. He studied hard and years later graduated from high school, he was the first African-American accepted into Iowa Agricultural College, where he studied Botany.

In 1896, Booker T. Washington recruited Carver to teach Botany at Tuskegee Institute's Agriculture School. During his train ride from Iowa to Alabama, Carver noticed the entire South badly needed a new agricultural technique. He discovered all of the farm land was worn out due to only growing cotton each year, this was very damaging to the soil and drained its nutrients. He began teaching his students a new groundbreaking method for crop rotation.

Invention: Carver advised all farmers to plant cotton one year, then peanuts and sweet potatoes the following year. Southern farmers followed his lead to great success. He also famously developed more than 300 uses from peanuts, from ink, to hand lotion, to cooking oil. In 1942, President Franklin D. Roosevelt left Washington D.C. to visit Tuskegee Institute's campus to personally greet Carver and applaud his remarkable research.

Carver also revolutionized the soybean, he developed more than 100 uses from soybeans, from plastic to adhesives. In 1942, Carver taught automotive pioneer Henry Ford how to construct a new line of automobile parts using plastic that was produced from soybeans. Carver and Ford became close friends, with Carver's advice, Ford created a 7000 acre soybean farm in Michigan.

Lewis Latimer

Inventions:

In 1881, Lewis Latimer invented a Carbon Filament for the Incandescent Lightbulb. His creation made electric lighting more practical and affordable for the average household, he was also directly involved with the invention of the Telephone. Latimer patented several other inventions including an improved Railroad Car Bathroom and an early Air Conditioning Unit. Latimer was inducted into the National Inventors Hall of Fame in 2006.

Lewis Latimer

(1848 – 1928)

Background: Lewis Latimer was born September 4, 1848 in Chelsea, Massachusetts. His parents were slaves who escaped from Virginia to seek freedom in Boston, MA. His father, George Latimer was tried in court for being a runaway in an extremely famous case, he was defended by abolitionist Frederick Douglas. After the trial, he was allowed to remain in Boston as a free man.

At the age of fifteen, Latimer enlisted in the Navy to serve in the Civil War. Once the war ended, he returned home to Boston. He taught himself the trade of mechanical drawing while working at a patent law firm. While at the firm, he completed many projects working with the famous Inventor Hiram Maxim from the U.S. Electric Lighting Company.

Latimer worked closely with Inventor Thomas Edison, he also drafted the drawings that Alexander Graham Bell used to patent the first Telephone in 1876.

Invention: Latimer made improvements to Edison's lightbulb, in 1881, he invented a carbon filament for the incandescent lightbulb which allowed lighting to become more efficient and affordable.

Latimer's abilities in electric lighting became well known, due to his expertise, he was sought after to continue the expansion of incandescent lighting. As more major cities began wiring their streets for electric lighting, Latimer was dispatched to lead the planning team.

He helped to install the first electric plants in many cities including Philadelphia, New York City and Montreal. He also oversaw the installation of lighting in railroad stations, government buildings and major thoroughfares in Canada, New England and London. Latimer was a brilliant innovator, he once mentioned his goal in life was to improve the lives of everyday people.

Garrett Morgan

Inventions:

Garrett Morgan invented the Gas Mask, Traffic Signal and a Hair Straightening Chemical later known as "Conk." Morgan's safety inventions have improved and saved countless lives worldwide, including firefighters, miners, soldiers and vehicle operators. His work paved the way for many modern day inventors and engineers. Morgan was inducted into the National Inventors Hall of Fame in 2005.

Garrett Morgan

(1877 – 1963)

Background: Garrett Morgan was born on March 4, 1877 in Paris, Kentucky. As a young man he moved to Cincinnati, Ohio to search for employment. While working at a textile factory, Morgan witnessed a huge fire engulf a factory building. When firefighters arrived on the scene, he noticed they were all struggling to withstand the suffocating smoke and other pollutants while trying to contain the fire.

Invention: In 1914, Morgan invented the "Safety Hood," a device which made polluted air breathable. The invention was an early version of the Gas Mask, later used in World War I to protect soldiers from poison gas.

His invention was famously put to use during a tragic event in Cleveland, Ohio. In 1916, a tunnel that was being drilled under Lake Erie suddenly collapsed, trapping 32 workers. Smoke and toxic fumes prevented firefighters from safely rescuing the workers. Morgan along with his brother used his safety hood to successfully reach the trapped men and rescue several survivors.

In 1923, Morgan invented the Traffic Signal, he was inspired to do so after he witnessed a serious car accident at a busy intersection. In those days, cars, bicycles, horse drawn vehicles and pedestrians all had to share the road simultaneously, which was often very dangerous.

Morgan's traffic signal was the first to feature three commands instead of two, which controlled traffic more effectively. In 1923, he sold the patent rights to General Electric for $40,000.00.

Morgan also diligently supported the African-American community throughout his lifetime, he was a member of the newly formed NAACP. In 1920, he also launched an African-American newspaper named the Cleveland Call.

Dr. Charles Richard Drew

Inventions:

Dr. Charles Drew was a Surgeon and Medical Researcher. He conducted research in the field of blood transfusions while developing improved techniques for blood storage. He also pioneered the first large-scale Blood Collection Program in the United States during World War II. In 1942, he patented an Apparatus for Preserving Blood. Dr. Drew was inducted into the National Inventors Hall of Fame in 2015.

African-American Inventions That Changed The World

Dr. Charles Richard Drew

(1904 – 1950)

Background: Dr. Charles Richard Drew was born on June 3, 1904 in Washington, D.C. As a young man, he was an athlete and honor student. He graduated from Amherst College before studying medicine at McGill University in Canada.

Invention: In the late 1930's, Dr. Drew invented a new way to process and preserve blood plasma, he designed and patented an apparatus that allowed blood to be stored and shipped in the event of it being needed for a transfusion. Prior to his invention, blood was perishable and not fit for use after about a week, his new method vastly improved the efficiency of blood banks.

Dr. Drew's work took on new urgency during World War II. As the leading expert on blood storage, he worked on a project with Great Britain to oversee blood banks for British troops. In 1941, he was named medical director of the American Red Cross National Blood Donor Service. He recruited and organized the collection of  thousands of pints of blood donations for American troops. It was the first mass blood collection program of its kind.

At the time, the U.S. Armed Forces segregated blood from African-American and Caucasian donors. Dr. Drew was outraged by this policy, he was frustrated and spoke out against this racist and unnecessary practice, the military refused to change their policy and he ultimately resigned. He then started working at Howard University, serving as a professor and the head of the department of surgery. Later in his career, Dr. Drew was the chief surgeon at Freedmen's Hospital. He was also the first African-American examiner for the American Board of Surgery.

Otis Boykin

Inventions:

Otis Boykin has 26 patents to his name, his most noteworthy invention was a Control Unit that would be later used for pacemakers. He also invented a Wire Precision Resistor that would later be used in radios, televisions and computers. Boykin was inducted into the National Inventors Hall of Fame in 2014.

Otis Boykin

(1920 – 1982)

Background: Otis Boykin was born on August 29, 1920 in Dallas, Texas. He attended Fisk College in Nashville, Tennessee, he later moved to Chicago and attended the Illinois Institute of Technology. After graduation, he accepted a position with P.J. Nilsen Research Laboratories while also trying to start his own business.

Boykin later decided to work for himself as an Inventor. He set out to work on a project that he once contemplated while he was in college, he developed a special talent in working with resistors. Resistors slow the flow of electricity, allowing a safe amount of electricity to move through a device.

Invention: In 1959, Boykin invented a Wire Precision Resistor, this device allowed specific amounts of electrical currents to flow for a specific purpose. He also created another type resistor that could withstand shifts in temperature and air pressure. All of his resistors lead to huge breakthroughs, allowing electronic devices to become affordable as well as more reliable than ever before.

His inventions were in great demand, he received hundreds of orders from Consumer Electronic Manufacturers, the United States Armed Forces as well as IBM.

Boykin had 26 patents to his name, the resistors he created were used in products like radios, televisions, computers and also military missiles.

His most noteworthy invention was a Control Unit that is used in pacemakers, which are small devices that doctors implant in the human body to help the heart beat normally. Boykin's invention allowed the pacemaker to be more precisely regulated, it is responsible for saving hundreds of thousands of lives each year.

Elijah McCoy

Inventions:

In 1872, Elijah McCoy invented an Automatic Lubricator for train engines, he also has nearly 60 more patents to his name. His inventions have enabled trains to run faster and more efficiently. McCoy was inducted into the National Inventors Hall of Fame in 2001.

Elijah McCoy

(1844 – 1929)

Background: Elijah McCoy was born on May 2, 1844 in Colchester, Ontario Canada. His parents were former slaves from Kentucky who escaped through the Underground Railroad into Canada. His family eventually returned back to the United States, settling in Michigan. At the age of fifteen, McCoy traveled to Scotland for an apprenticeship in mechanical engineering. When he returned back home to Michigan, he was unable to find work as an engineer, due to racial barriers.

Despite his qualifications, skilled professional positions were not available for African-Americans at the time. He then accepted a position as a fireman working with the Michigan Central Railroad. One of his duties was oiling steam engine parts on trains. McCoy noticed the oiling process had to be completed very often, it also required the train to stop each time. He pondered how he could create a more effective way to complete this process.

Invention: In 1872, McCoy invented an Automatic Lubricator. This device allowed oil to be evenly distributed through train engine parts while still in motion. His lubricator also allowed trains to run for longer periods of time without stopping for maintenance, which saved the railroad industry both time and money.

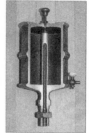

McCoy was a prolific inventor, he completely changed the travel industry with his work on the steam engine. Along with his automatic lubricator, he secured nearly 60 other patents in his lifetime.

As his reputation as an inventor grew in popularity, inferior counterfeits to his original inventions began to emerge. Railway engineers started requesting "The Real McCoy" when they needed to replace steam engine parts. The popular expression, meaning "The Real Thing" has also stood the test of time, more than a century later the phrase continues to be used today.

Madam C.J. Walker

Inventions:

Madam C.J. Walker invented the Hot Comb and a line of African-American hair care products. She was an Entrepreneur, Philanthropist, Political and Social Activist. Her savvy business talent led her to become the first woman in the United States to be a self-made millionaire.

Madam C.J. Walker

(1867 – 1919)

Background: Madam C.J. Walker was born Sarah Breedlove on December 23, 1867 in Delta, Louisiana to former enslaved parents. Walker was orphaned when she was seven years old, at the age of twenty, she moved to St. Louis, Missouri and later married Charles J. Walker.

Invention: During the early 1890's, Walker began to suffer from a scalp ailment which resulted in her losing her hair. She began to experiment with various products that she purchased along with some homemade remedies. She eventually created a scalp conditioning and healing formula that worked for her (claiming it was revealed to her in a dream). She named her new formula, "Madame C.J. Walker's Wonderful Hair Grower."

In 1906, she changed her name to Madam C.J. Walker and marketed herself as an independent hairdresser and retailer of cosmetic creams. She adopted the name "Madam" from women pioneers of the French Beauty Industry.

Walker traveled around the country promoting her products along with hair care tips to African-American women. Her talent for self-promotion made her one of the most famous African-Americans of her time and a very successful businesswoman. She was also the first woman in the United States to become a self-made millionaire.

Walker made financial contributions to many organizations, while donating generously to African-American causes, she also took pride in employing thousands of "hair culturists," who helped sell her products. Her lavish New York estate "Villa Lewaro," served as a social gathering place for the African-American community. In 1927, the City of Indianapolis, IN. honored her legacy, opening "The Madame Walker Theatre Center," both of these iconic properties are listed on the national register of historic places.

Alexander Miles

Inventions:

In 1887, Alexander Miles invented a method for opening and closing elevator doors automatically. This new automated process dramatically improved passenger safety and saved countless lives. Miles was inducted into the National Inventors Hall of Fame in 2007.

Alexander Miles

(1838 – 1918)

Background: Alexander Miles was born on May 18, 1838 in Ohio. In 1876, he and his family moved to Duluth, Minnesota.

When elevators were first invented in the mid-19th century, passengers or conductors had to manually open and close the elevator doors as well as the door leading directly down the shaft. This process made riding an elevator extremely dangerous.

Earlier elevator models were not designed for passenger safety, if someone failed to close the door leading to the shaft when exiting, another passenger could possibly fall down the shaft while attempting to step into the elevator.

One day while riding an elevator with his young daughter, Miles realized the imminent danger his children faced associated with an elevator shaft door being carelessly left open. This event inspired him to draft a design for automated elevator doors.

Invention: In 1887, Miles invented an automated mechanism that allowed shaft doors along with the elevator doors to open and close automatically on each floor, this new method allowed passengers to have a much safer ride. The elevators we ride today still feature the same mechanism similar to his invention.

Along with being an inventor, Miles was also a successful businessman, he worked as a real estate investor and a barber. He was the first African-American chamber of commerce member in Duluth, Minnesota. In 1900, Miles moved to Chicago, Illinois and founded his own insurance company. He wanted to help African-Americans who experienced discriminatory treatment with other insurance companies. All of his achievements and success led him to become the wealthiest man in the pacific northwest region of the United States during the early 1900's.

Jan Ernst Matzeliger

Inventions:

In 1883, Jan Ernst Matzeliger invented an automatic Shoe Making Machine. His machine was able to create hundreds of pairs of shoes in a single day, vastly increasing production in the shoe making industry. On September 15, 1991, the United States Postal Service honored Matzeliger on the Black Heritage U.S.A Postage Stamp. He was also inducted into the National Inventors Hall of Fame in 2006.

Jan Ernst Matzeliger

(1852 – 1889)

Background: Jan Ernst Matzeliger was born on September 15, 1852 in Dutch Guiana, the South American country now called Suriname. In his early years, he worked in a machine shop that was supervised by his father. At the age of nineteen, Matzeliger left Suriname on a voyage to explore the world, he worked as a mechanic on a Dutch East Indies merchant ship for several years before settling in Philadelphia, Pennsylvania in 1877.

When Matzeliger first arrived in Philadelphia, he learned the shoe trade. He later moved to Lynn, Massachusetts where he found work as an apprentice in a shoe factory. He then learned the trade of cordwaining, which involves crafting shoes almost entirely by hand.

Cordwainer's create molds of their customers feet (known as "lasts") using wood or stone. Shoes were then sized and shaped according to the molds, this was considered the most difficult and time consuming stage of assembly. A skilled cordwainer could produce about 50 pairs of shoes in a day.

Invention: In 1883, Matzeliger successfully invented what many before him attempted, but failed to complete. He created an automatic Shoemaking Machine that could quickly attach the top of the shoe to the sole (a process known as "lasting"). His machine could produce more than 10 times what human hands could create in a single day. This invention revolutionized the shoemaking industry and made shoes more affordable for the average person.

Matzeliger's machine could produce between 500 and 700 pairs of shoes in a day, cutting shoe prices across the nation in half. His invention paved the way for modern day shoe manufacturers who can produce tens of thousands of shoes per day.

Granville T. Woods

Inventions:

In 1887, Granville T. Woods invented the Multiplex Telegraph. This device allowed train operators to communicate with each other, it also helped them avoid collisions and other dangers on the tracks. Woods made railways much safer, he has nearly 60 patents to his name and he revolutionized the railroad industry. Woods was inducted into the National Inventors Hall of Fame in 2006.

African-American Inventions That Changed The World

Granville T. Woods

(1856 – 1910)

Background: Granville T. Woods was born on April 23, 1856 in Columbus, Ohio to a Native-American mother and an African-American father. As a young man, he worked as a railroad worker and engineer. Prior to his invention, train collisions were a common occurrence and a huge problem. As an engineer, Woods constantly tried to figure new ways to improve the railroad industry.

Invention: In 1887, Woods invented the Multiplex Telegraph. This device allowed dispatchers and engineers to communicate with train conductors via telegraph wires, helping them to avoid dangers on the tracks. This device also allowed conductors to communicate with their counterparts on other trains. His invention transformed the railroad industry, preventing future railroad collisions as well as passenger deaths from occurring.

Woods held nearly 60 other patents throughout his lifetime. Many of these inventions were for electric railways. The "Third Rail," which uses electricity to pull trains forward, was another one of his inventions that is still widely used today.

One of his most noted inventions was the "Trolley," a metal grooved wheel that allowed street cars to collect electric power from overhead wires. Woods also improved the Automatic Air-Brakes used on railroad cars.

In 1884, Woods invented the Advanced Telephone Transmitter. This device was an advancement of Alexander Graham Bell's famous telephone invention. Bell's company purchased the rights from Woods for this device, fearing he would become one of their major competitors. Along with American Bell Telephone Company, many of his other inventions were sold to other major companies like General Electric and The Westinghouse Electric Company.

Dr. George Franklin Grant

Inventions:

In 1899, Dr. George Franklin Grant invented the world's first Golf Tee. He also invented a medical device called the Oblate Palate.

Dr. George Franklin Grant

(1846 - 1910)

Background: Dr. George Franklin Grant was born on September 15, 1846 in Oswego, New York to former enslaved parents. When he was fifteen years old, he was hired as a lab assistant by a local dentist. After a few years of learning the business, he was encouraged to pursue his own career in dentistry. In 1868, Dr. Grant became the first African-American student to enter the Harvard School of Dental Medicine.

After graduation, Dr. Grant accepted a position in the Department of Mechanical Dentistry in 1871, making him Harvard University's first African-American faculty member. Dr. Grant was an avid golfer, prior to his invention, golfers frequently carried around buckets of sand on golf courses.

They used the sand to build a small mound, in order to place the golf ball on before each stroke. This was an extremely messy and time consuming process. Dr. Grant pondered a solution for this problem.

Invention: In 1899, he invented the world's first Golf Tee. His device was whittled from wood and capped with gutta-percha, which is a latex resin used in dentistry for root canals. The popularity of his invention grew very quickly, golfers were finally able to play 18 holes of golf without the burden of carrying around sand buckets.

As a dentist, Dr. Grant specialized in treating patients with congenital cleft palates, which is a birth defect that occurs when a baby's lip or mouth does not form properly. In 1899, he invented the Oblate Palate, a prosthetic device that dentist use to allow patients with a cleft palate to speak normally.

Benjamin Banneker

Inventions:

In 1753, Benjamin Banneker invented the first Clock in the United States at the age of twenty-one. He also surveyed and designed the plans for the layout of Washington D.C. Banneker was a Scientist and Author, he created a popular series of Almanacs. On February 15, 1980, the United States Postal Service honored Banneker on the Black Heritage U.S.A Postage Stamp.

Benjamin Banneker

(1731 - 1806)

Background: Benjamin Banneker was born November 9, 1731 in Baltimore, Maryland to enslaved parents. Growing up, he was allowed to enroll in school. He excelled in his studies, particularly in mathematics and science. Banneker progressed far beyond the capabilities of his teachers, he had a reputation for solving very complex math problems.

One day his family was introduced to a man who owned a pocket watch named Josef Levi. Young Benjamin was so fascinated by the object, Levi gave it to him to keep as a gift and explained how it worked. Over the course of the next few days, Banneker repeatedly took the watch apart and then put it back together. He read dozens books on geometry and made plans to build a larger version of the watch.

Invention: After two years of designing and carving each piece by hand including the gears, Banneker successfully created the first clock ever built in the United States. The clock was amazingly precise and it kept perfect time for the next thirty years. As a result, he opened his own watch and clock repair business.

Banneker was also fascinated with the stars in the sky, he developed a strong passion for astronomy. He began reading different books on astronomy while using telescopes to study the sky. He was soon able to predict events such as a solar eclipse along with sunrises and sunsets each day. In 1792, he wrote his first Almanac, he later authored five more publications. His almanacs were in great demand and they all sold very well.

In 1791, President George Washington decided to move the nation's capitol from Philadelphia to an area on the border of Maryland and Virginia. Banneker was asked to assist with surveying and designing the territory, the plans and designs he drew up were the basis for the layout of Washington D.C. Many of the buildings and monuments he designed still exist today.

Gerald Lawson

Inventions:

Gerald Lawson invented the world's first Home Video Gaming System that used interchangeable cartridges.

Gerald Lawson

(1940 - 2011)

Background: Gerald Lawson was born on December 1, 1940 in Brooklyn, New York. While growing up, both of his parents encouraged his interest in scientific hobbies. He later developed a talent working with computers and electronics. Lawson earned a living repairing television sets while in college. He attended both Queens College and City College of New York.

His talent in computing led him in the 1970's to Silicon Valley's Homebrew Computer Club. Two of his peers that were members of the club were Steve Jobs and Steve Wozniak, the future co-founders of Apple, Incorporated.

Invention: Lawson pioneered the home video game industry in the 1970's, he created The Fairchild Channel F. Video Entertainment Computer. This device was the world's first ROM based cartridge video game console system with interchangeable cartridges.

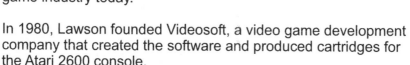

This new technology allowed video gaming companies to sell individual games separately from the console itself, which is a business model that remains the cornerstone of the video game industry today.

In 1980, Lawson founded Videosoft, a video game development company that created the software and produced cartridges for the Atari 2600 console.

Lawson's ingenuity allowed many new video game manufacturing companies to follow his lead to great success. Over the past three decades, the video game industry has generated more revenue than the film industry, it has evolved into a one-hundred billion dollar industry worldwide.

Benjamin F. Thornton

Inventions:

In 1935, Benjamin F. Thornton invented the world's first Telephone Answering Machine.

Benjamin F. Thornton

Background: Benjamin F. Thornton's exact birthdate and birthplace are unknown, there is not much known about his early personal life. He was living in Harrisburg, Pennsylvania when he designed his famous invention.

In the 1930's, the telephone was a very popular device, the technology was fairly new and many people during this time experienced owning one for the first time. Although this device was very convenient, it had a few shortcomings.

There were many occasions when telephone owners had to wait around for an entire day if they were expecting an important phone call. There was also the uncertainty of not knowing if expected phone calls were missed altogether.

Recognizing these concerns, Thornton had an idea of creating a recording system that allowed a caller to leave a voice recorded message in the event of the recipient being away from their home or office.

Invention: In 1935, Thornton invented the world's first Telephone Answering Machine. This device was able to record multiple telephone messages from several callers using a turntable along with a recordable record. The device also featured an electric motor as well as an electric switch that was connected directly to the telephone line.

Thornton's device was equipped with a clock attachment in order to keep track of the time each call was received, every message received was stamped in chronological order. Recorded messages even had the ability of being forwarded to other telephones. His invention forever changed the way people communicated over the telephone.

Thornton's groundbreaking invention paved the way for many modern day telephone message recoding devices. There are an estimated five billion voice messages recorded around the world each day on devices such as answering machines and voicemail.

Dr. Patricia Bath

Inventions:

Dr. Patricia Bath is an Ophthalmologist and Laser Scientist. In 1981, she invented the Laserphaco Probe, a medical tool that is used by doctors during eye surgery to correct cataracts. Her laser device has helped restore and improve vision for millions of people worldwide.

Dr. Patricia Bath

(1942 – 2019)

Background: Dr. Patricia Bath was born on November 4, 1942 in Harlem, New York. Dr. Bath attended Medical School at Howard University and completed her fellowship at Columbia University. She completed her training at New York University School of Medicine, making her the first African-American to complete a residency in Ophthalmology.

In 1974, Dr. Bath joined the faculty of UCLA and Charles R. Drew University as an assistant Professor of Ophthalmology and Surgery. During her tenure, she had to break through many racial and gender barriers. Dr. Bath began researching and developing a model for a laser instrument for the removal of cataracts. She decided to take her research abroad to the Laser Medical Center of Berlin, West Germany, the Rothschild Eye Institute of Paris, France, and the Loughborough Institute of Technology in England.

Invention: In 1981, Dr. Bath invented a surgical tool called the Laserphaco Probe. This device is a medical tool doctors use during eye surgery to correct cataracts. Dr. Bath was awarded a U.S. patent in 1988, she also holds patents in Japan, Canada and Europe.

Cataracts is a clouding of the eye's natural lens which leads to a decrease in vision or blindness, it can often develop slowly and can affect one or both eyes, many elderly people suffer from cataracts.

Her laser tool is more precise, less invasive and less risky than previous devices that were used during cataracts surgeries. Dr. Bath was able to help restore the sight of individuals who were blind for more than 30 years using her Laserphaco Probe.

Dr. Bath is the first African-American female doctor to secure a medical patent. In 1976, she co-founded the American Institute for the Prevention of Blindness, which established that "eyesight is a basic human right."

Dr. Henry T. Sampson

Inventions:

In 1971, Dr. Henry T. Sampson co-invented the Gamma-Electric Cell, this invention made it possible for cell phone technology to exist. Dr. Sampson also pioneered the study of internal ballistics of solid rocket motors using high speed photography.

Dr. Henry T. Sampson

(1934 – 2015)

Background: Dr. Henry T. Sampson's exact birthdate is unknown, he was born in Jackson, Mississippi in 1934. He earned a Master's Degree in Chemical Engineering from UCLA in 1961.

He continued his graduate studies and pursued a Doctoral Degree in Nuclear Engineering from the University of Illinois at Urbana-Champaign. In 1967, Dr. Sampson became the first African-American to earn a PhD in Nuclear Engineering in the United States.

Invention: In 1971, Dr. Sampson co-invented the Gamma-Electric Cell, a direct-conversion energy device that converts the energy generated from gamma rays into electricity. His revolutionary invention made it possible for cell phone technology to exist.

On April 3, 1973, the first ever cell phone call was placed in Midtown Manhattan, New York City. Dr. Sampson's new gamma-electric cell technology was used during the call.

The call was placed on a Motorola DynaTAC 8000x, which weighed 2.5 pounds, a much heavier phone compared to average 3 ounce cell phones used today. The prototype offered a talk time of about 20 minutes and it took 10 hours to recharge.

Ever since that first call was placed, the cell phone has become a global phenomenon. There are currently more active mobile devices in the world than there are people. There are an estimated seventy-five billion cell phone calls made each day worldwide.

Sarah E. Goode

Inventions:

Sarah E. Goode is the first African-American woman to receive a U.S. patent. In 1885, she invented the Folding Cabinet Bed.

Sarah E. Goode

(1855 - 1905)

Background: Sarah E. Goode was born Sarah Elisabeth Jacobs in Toledo, Ohio in 1855, her exact birthdate is unknown. Goode was born into slavery, she received her freedom at the end of the Civil War. She then moved to Chicago, Illinois where she met Archibald "Archie" Goode. The couple married and had six children.

While living in Chicago, Goode become an entrepreneur, she opened a furniture store on Chicago's South Side. Many of her customers were working-class people who lived in small homes or studios. They had a minimal amount of living space and expressed their concern of not having enough room to add furniture.

Goode had an idea of creating a piece of furniture that would served multiple uses, her device would allow people to utilize the space in their homes more efficiently.

Invention: Goode invented the Folding Cabinet Bed. This piece of furniture was a bed that could be converted into a desk.

When the bed was not being used, it included a mechanism to completely transform it into a roll-top desk complete with compartments for stationery along with writing supplies. Her invention is the predecessor of the Murphy Bed.

Goode received a patent for her invention in 1885, making her the first African-American woman to be awarded a U.S. Patent.

In 2012, The City of Chicago honored Goode with opening a new school on the south side with her namesake, the "Sarah E. Goode STEM Academy." Attendees of the school are not called students, but rather "Innovators". Their curriculum prepares them for jobs in the fields of science, technology, engineering and mathematics.

George Murray

Inventions:

George Murray held many titles, Farmer, Teacher, Land Developer and Federal Customs Inspector. He was a former slave who later became an Inventor as well as a United States Congressman. He invented the Fertilizer Distributor and the Cotton Chopper, he was awarded several other patents for farming tools.

George Murray

(1853 - 1926)

Background: George Murray was born on September 22, 1853 in Sumter County, South Carolina. He spent the first thirteen years of his life as a slave. Once he was emancipated, he aspired to receive a formal education. Murray then enrolled at South Carolina State University.

Invention: All of Murray's inventions were a result of him being a farmer, his goal was to lessen some of the intense labor that was involved in farming. In 1894, he invented the Seed Furrow Opener. This device allowed farmers to create a well-defined groove in the soil where seeds could be placed at a proper depth.

Another device he invented the Stalk-Knocker Cultivator, which was designed to speed up the planting and harvesting process. In 1894, Murray also patented several other inventions included the Fertilizer Distributor and the Cotton Chopper.

Throughout Murray's professional career, he was a school teacher, chairman of the Sumter County Republican Committee and a federal customs inspector for the port of Charleston, South Carolina.

In 1892, Murray was elected to the United States Congress, representing the State of South Carolina. He was the only African-American Congressman to hold a seat in the 53rd and 54th Congresses. He focused his efforts on protecting African-American voting rights in the South during a time when a growing number of African-American voters were being excluded from the polls. He was also a member of the House Committee of Education.

Murray frequently spoke on the floor of the House, describing the plight of African-American citizens throughout the country, he implored his fellow congressmen to uphold the law of the land and began protecting their rights as equal citizens of the United States.

Dr. Thomas Elkins

Inventions:

In 1879, Dr. Thomas Elkins invented the improved Refrigerator. He also made improvements to the Toilet and Dining Room Table designs.

Dr. Thomas Elkins

Background: Dr. Thomas Elkins exact birthdate is unknown, he was born in the early 1800's in Albany, New York. Dr. Elkins was a pharmacist and a respected member of the Albany community.

Prior to his famous invention, the most common way of keeping perishable items fresh was placing them into an icebox container surrounded by large blocks of ice. Over time the ice would eventually melt and the food would began to spoil. Dr. Elkins wanted create a new apparatus that allowed people to preserve their perishable items for more than a couple of days.

Invention: In 1879, he invented the improved Refrigerator. This device utilized metal cooling coils that became very cold, it produced cool air that filled an enclosed area within a sealed refrigerated box.

His device included a vacuumed sealed door that was designed to keep cool air inside, which allowed perishable items inside to remain fresh for longer periods of time.

In 1872, Dr. Elkins also invented the improved Chamber Commode (Toilet). His commode design was a combination bureau, mirror, book-rack, washstand, table, easy chair, and chamber stool. It was a very unusual piece of furniture. His innovation led to many modern day toilet designs that are still in use today.

Dr. Elkins was also an abolitionist. He was the secretary of the "Vigilance Committee," an anti-slavery organization that formed in many northern cities in the early 1840's. They protected freedom seekers from re-enslavement. To assist them in their flight to freedom, these "Vigilance Committees" provided legal assistance, food, clothing, money, employment, and temporary shelter.

Marie Van Brittan Brown

Inventions:

In 1969, Marie Van Brittan Brown invented the world's first Home Security System, she also invented the first ever Closed Circuit Television.

Marie Van Brittan Brown

(1922 - 1999)

Background: Marie Van Brittan Brown was born on October 22, 1922 in Queens, New York. Brown was instrumental in the creation of the Home Security Surveillance System. Due to her profession as a registered nurse, Brown worked irregular hours, which left her home alone many times.

When the crime rate in her neighborhood spiked, Brown feared for he personal safety, she decided to create home monitoring system that allowed her to feel safe while home alone. Her invention was inspired by the security risk her home faced.

Invention: In 1969, Brown invented the world's first Home Security System. Her invention was comprised of a camera, peepholes, monitors, and a two way microphone. There was also an alarm button that she could press to contact the police in the event of an emergency.

There was a surveillance camera attached to the opposite side of her front door that had the capability of sliding up and down, the camera picked up images that would reflect on a monitor via a wireless system. The monitor could be placed in any part of the house, allowing her to see who was at the door.

There was also a voice component feature that allowed her to speak to the person outside of there front door, if the person was perceived to be an intruder, the police would be notified when the alarm button was pressed, if the person was a welcomed or expected visitor, the door could be unlocked via remote control.

Due to Brown's innovation, there are millions of homeowners who now entrust home security systems to protect their families and homes in the event of a home invasion, fire or medical emergency.

Richard Spikes

Inventions:

Richard Spikes has 26 patents to his name, his most noteworthy invention was the Automatic Transmission Gear Shifting Device. In 1913, he also invented the improvement of the Automobile Directional Signal. Many of his diverse inventions include:

Railroad semaphore (1906)
Beer keg tap (1910)
Self-locking rack for billiard cues (1910)
Automatic car washer (1913)
Automobile directional signals (1913)
Continuous contact trolley pole (1919)
Brake testing machine (1923)
Combination milk bottle opener and cover (1926)
Transmission gear shift (1933)
Automatic shoe shine chair (1939)
Multiple barrel machine gun (1940)
Horizontally swinging barber chair (1950)
Automatic safety brake system (1962)

Richard Spikes

(1878 - 1963)

Background: Richard Spikes was born on October 2, 1878 in Dallas Texas. He was an engineer and a prolific inventor, over a 60 year span he patented 26 of his inventions.

Spikes dedicated much of his life to creating devices that made life much easier for future generations. Most his inventions were incredibly popular and recognized by many major corporations who were interested in purchasing them.

Invention: In 1910, Spikes invented the Beer Keg Tap. This device was later purchased and implemented by the Milwaukee Brewing Beer Company. Spikes was a very diverse inventor, several of his creations were designed for the automobile industry.

In 1913, he invented the improved Automobile Directional Signals. Pierce Arrow Automobiles was interested in his design, they added this new technology to their new line of cars, which soon became the industry standard for all new automobiles manufactured in the United States.

In 1933, Spikes also invented the Automatic Transmission Gear Shift. This device is now standard on all automobiles with a manual transmission, he sold the patent rights for this invention to a major automobile manufacturer for $100,000.00 in 1934.

While attempting to create his Automatic Safety Brake System design, Spikes sadly began to lose his vision. He was determined to complete this project and did not allow this handicap to slow him down, he first invented a Drafting Machine for blind engineers.

Once he completed his safety brake invention in 1962, it became industry standard for all new manufactured automobiles and school buses in the United States.

Philip Downing

Inventions:

In 1891, Philip Downing invented the Street Letter Box, which is known today as the Mailbox. He also invented an Electrical Switch System used on railroads. Downing was elected as a member of the Wisconsin State Senate in 1940.

Philip Downing

(1871 - 1961)

Background: Philip Downing was born on September 3, 1871 in Fenaghvale, Ontario, Canada. At the age of twelve, he and his family moved from Canada to Boston, Massachusetts. In his early years, Downing developed a talent in engineering and mechanics.

During the 19th Century, the most common way for people to communicate with someone who lived far away was writing a letter. The only way to send a letter during those days was taking it down to the local post office.

Downing had an idea of designing an apparatus that would allow people to securely place outgoing letters in a protected community postal box centrally located in their neighborhood. This box would serve as a convenient alternative to going to the post office.

Invention: In 1891, Downing invented the Street Letter Box, which is the predecessor to the mailbox. His design featured a steel frame along with a hinging door that was supported by four legs. The distinctive steel frame design provided a safeguard for letters against elements such as snow, rain and dirt. He also wanted to provide a deterrent from theft.

Over a century later, Downing's invention has forever changed the way mail is handled, it's estimated that millions of letters are processed and delivered through the United States Postal Service each year. The street letter mailbox handles a significant portion of that volume.

In 1890, Downing also invented an Electrical Switch System for railroads. This device allowed workers to supply power or shut down power to trains at the appropriate times. Based on his design, this device inspired future innovators to later create the "electrical light switch," similar to the ones used in homes today.

Along with being an inventor, Downing also had a successful career in politics. He served as a member of the Wisconsin State Senate 30th district from 1941 until 1956.

Dr. Daniel Hale Williams

Inventions:

In 1893, Dr. Daniel Hale Williams became the first Surgeon in the United States to successfully perform an Open Heart Surgery.

Dr. Daniel Hale Williams

(1856 - 1931)

Background: Dr. Daniel Hale Williams was born on January 18, 1856 in Hollidaysburg, Pennsylvania. He moved to Chicago, Illinois with his family at a young age. Growing up, he wanted to become a doctor. Dr. Williams worked as an apprentice for a highly accomplished surgeon in the Chicago area, he then completed further training at Chicago Medical College.

When Dr. Williams graduated from Medical School in 1883, he opened his own medical practice in Chicago. African-American doctors were not allowed to work in Chicago area hospitals in those days. Dr. Williams was highly regarded as a skilled surgeon, his practice grew because he treated people of all races. In 1883, he opened Provident Hospital, an interracial facility established to provide medical attention for all citizens.

In 1893, a patient named James Cornish was admitted due to a lethal stab wound he sustained to his chest, at the time operating on a human heart was extremely dangerous and there was no precedent for opening the chest.

Invention: Although he did not have the benefits of penicillin, antibiotics, x-rays, adequate anesthesia or other tools used in modern surgery, Dr. Williams was faced with opening Cornish's chest and operating internally. He then performed surgery to repair a tear in the lining of Cornish's heart, this was the first successful open heart surgery performed in the United States.

James Cornish fully recovered and would go on to live for another 50 years. Dr. Williams work as a pioneering surgeon has paved the way for modern day doctors who frequently perform the open heart surgery procedure and save countless lives worldwide.

George Crum

Inventions:

In 1853, George Crum invented Potato Chips.

George Crum

(1822 - 1926)

Background: George Crum was born George Speck on July 15, 1822 in Saratoga Lake, New York to a Native-American mother and an African-American father. As an adult he adopted the professional name "Crum," a name his father also used as a jockey. In his early years, Crum worked as a mountain guide in the Adirondacks, he later recognized his talent with food preparation and became a professional chef.

Invention: In 1853, Crum was working as a chef in a restaurant at the Moon Lake Lodge, a resort in Saratoga Springs, New York. One day while preparing meals in the kitchen, a patron sent back the restaurant's popular french fried potatoes dish, complaining that the potatoes were cut too thick. Although Crum prepared a second thinner batch, the patron was still very unsatisfied.

An annoyed Crum, sliced a new batch of potatoes as thin as he possibly could and fried them until they were completely hard and crunchy, he then added a generous amount of salt to them. He was surprised to find out the patron actually enjoyed the new dish he invented, at that moment "Potato Chips" were born.

Years later, Crum opened his own restaurant. He had a basket of potato chips on every table, he named them "Saratoga Chips" or "Potato Crunches," his customers fell in love with them. His potato chip snack was an enormous success and a customer favorite.

Unfortunately, Crum never attempted to patent his potato chip invention or sought to market them outside of his restaurant.

His invention was eventually marketed by others, then mass produced. More than a century later, Crum's invention has evolved into a seven billion dollar a year industry. Potato chips have evolved into one of the world's most popular snack foods.

John Albert Burr

Inventions:

John Albert Burr held over 30 patents for Lawn Care and Agricultural inventions. Most of his inventions were centered on easing the burden of farm workers and laborers. In 1899, he invented the improved Rotary Blade Lawn Mower.

African-American Inventions That Changed The World

John Albert Burr

(1848 - 1926)

Background: John Albert Burr's exact birthdate is unknown, he was born in Maryland in 1848 to enslaved parents who were later free after the emancipation proclamation. In his early years Burr worked on a farm as a field hand.

His talent of working with farm equipment was recognized by some local wealthy African-American activists who ensured he would be able to attend engineering classes at a private university.

After his graduation, Burr put his mechanical skills to work making a living repairing and servicing farm equipment along with other machines.

Invention: In 1899, he invented the improved Rotary Lawnmower. His design was intended to prevent the clogging that plagued other mowers at the time. This device was more maneuverable, capable of mowing closer to buildings and clipping around objects such as lawn posts.

Burr continued to patent improvements to his design, he invented attachments for sifting and dispersing mulch clippings.

His rotary lawnmower invention revolutionized lawn care, it paved the way for future lawn mower designs which helped ease the work load of millions of laborers for generations to come.

Unlike many inventors who unfortunately never witnessed their designs become commercialized, Burr held over 30 U.S. patents. He enjoyed the fruits of his success by receiving royalties for many of his inventions.

Frederick McKinley Jones

Inventions:

In 1939, Frederick McKinley Jones invented Refrigerated Trucks. He also has over 60 patents to his name, the majority pertain to refrigeration technologies. His others are related to x-ray machines, engines and sound equipment. Jones was inducted into the National Inventors Hall of Fame in 2007.

Frederick McKinley Jones

(1893 - 1961)

Background: Frederick McKinley Jones was born on May 17, 1893 in Cincinnati, Ohio to an African-American mother and a Caucasian father. In his early years, Jones developed a talent in mechanics, he made a living repairing radio transmitters, personal radios and also motion picture devices.

A local businessman named Joseph A. Numero, who was also a film producer hired Jones to improve the sound equipment he used in his studio. Numero was very impressed by his ingenuity.

Invention: Jones was later presented with an opportunity to develop an apparatus that would allow large trucks to transport perishable items without them spoiling. In 1939, he invented a Portable Air Cooling Unit. This device allowed trucks to be refrigerated.

Jones and Numero formed a partnership, together they founded the U.S. Thermo Control Company. The company's popularity grew during World War II, his invention allowed the U.S. Military to preserve blood, medicine and food. These items could now be transported in refrigerated trucks to soldiers in need of them.

The Thermo Control Company also revolutionized the shipping and grocery businesses. Grocery chains were finally able to import and export perishable products instead of the regular canned goods. As a result, the frozen food industry was born, consumers were now able to enjoy fresh foods from around the country for the first time. Jones invention of the refrigerated truck allowed U.S. Thermo to become a multi-million dollar company.

Jones has over 60 patents to his name. In 1939, he invented an Automatic Ticket Dispensing Machine, he later sold the patent rights to RCA. This device was later used in all movie theaters.

Thomas Jennings

Inventions:

Thomas Jennings is the first African-American man to receive a U.S. patent. In 1821, he invented Dry Cleaning. Jennings was also inducted into the National Inventors Hall of Fame in 2015.

Thomas Jennings

(1791 - 1856)

Background: Thomas Jennings birthdate is unknown, he was born in 1791 in New York City as a free man. Jennings had a successful career as a tailor, he was a respected member of his community and his reputation as a tailor grew over the years. He eventually opened his own store in Manhattan on Church Street and it grew into one of the largest clothing stores in New York City.

Many of his customers were concerned and dismayed when the fabric on their clothing became soiled. Conventional methods of cleaning would often ruin the fabric, leaving the person to either continue wearing the items in their soiled condition or simply discard them.

Although, Jennings would have earned a profit simply creating and selling brand new clothing to replace the soiled items, he hated to see garments he previously created discarded.

Invention: He began experimenting with different solutions and cleaning agents, he tested them on various fabrics until he found the right combination to effectively clean them. In 1821, Jennings invented a method called "Dry-Scouring," also known today as Dry-Cleaning. His method of cleaning garments with an organic solvent that doesn't include water has stood the test of time for the past two centuries. The dry-cleaning business continues to be the cornerstone of all neighborhoods in every major city worldwide.

Jennings was also an Abolitionist and an active leader in his community who worked for African-American civil rights. In 1854, his daughter Elizabeth was arrested and forcibly removed from a "whites only" streetcar in New York City. Jennings helped arrange a legal defense for her and organized a movement against racial segregation on New York City public transportation.

The case went to the Supreme Court and she was defended by an attorney named Chester A. Arthur. Elizabeth won her case the following year in 1855. Her attorney Chester A. Arthur went on to become the 21st President of the United States.

Henry Blair

Inventions:

Henry Blair is the second African-American man to receive a U.S. patent. In 1834, he invented the Corn Seed Planter. He also invented the Cotton Planter in 1836.

Henry Blair

(1804 - 1860)

Background: Henry Blair's birthdate is unknown, he was born in 1804 in Glen Ross, Maryland.

There is not much known about Blair's personal life or family background other than he was a free man. During those days, slaves were not allowed to apply for U.S. patents.

Invention: In 1834, Blair invented the Corn Seed Planter. This apparatus allowed farmers to plant their corn more than 30 times faster than manually planting by hand, which saved a tremendous amount of time and eased the burden of labor. This device also served as a tool for weed control.

In 1936, Blair also invented the Cotton Planter. This device was a similar design to the corn seed planter in the way it was assembled. Both of his revolutionary inventions contributed to boosting the agricultural productivity in the South, transforming its economy.

These two inventions both worked by splitting the ground with two blades similar to shovels, which were pulled along by a mule. A wheel driven cylinder followed behind which dropped the seed into the newly plowed ground, then covered it back with soil. Blair is the second African-American to receive a U.S. patent for his inventions.

He was not an educated man and he did not know how to read or write. During the time he filed his two patent applications, Blair had to sign them with the letter "X" being that he unable to write his name.

Blair is the only inventor that received a patent from the United States Patent and Trade Office to be identified as a "Colored Man." No other inventor has ever been identified by their race.

William Purvis

Inventions:

In 1890, William Purvis invented the improvement to the Fountain Pen. He also invented the Hand Stamp, Bag Fastener and a Paper Bag making Machine.

William Purvis

(1838 - 1914)

Background: William Purvis was born on August 12, 1838 in Philadelphia, Pennsylvania. There is not much known about his early personal life. He was living in Philadelphia when he designed his famous invention.

Traditional pens from the early 1800s were called "Dip Pens." These pens were not equipped with ink reservoirs, they required the user to carry around a bottle filled with ink (know as an inkwell). In order to write or draw with the dip pen, it needed to be recharged or dipped first into the inkwell by the user.

Purvis wanted to eliminate this time consuming and messy process, he was interested in creating a device that was much more convenient than using dip pens.

Invention: In 1890, Purvis invented the improved Fountain Pen. This device featured a reservoir for storing ink within the pen that was fed to the tip. This device also included an elastic tube between the pens tip and reservoir which had a suction action to return excess ink back inside of the reservoir, reducing ink spills and increasing the longevity of the pen.

His invention was an instant hit and its popularity grew very quickly. Many professionals and lawmakers now had a durable and inexpensive pen they could carry in their pocket and use to sign contracts or fill out legal papers.

In 1894, Purvis also invented two machines for making paper bags, which he later sold to the Union Paper Bag Company of New York.

He also invented a Bag Fastener, a Self-Inking Hand Stamp and several devices for electric railroads. Purvis invented, but did not patent other items such as the edge cutter found on aluminum foil, cling wrap and wax paper boxes.

Jack Johnson

Inventions:

Jack Johnson was the first African-American Heavyweight Champion of the World. In 1922, he invented the Wrench.

Jack Johnson

(1878 - 1946)

Background: Born John Arthur Johnson on March 31, 1878 in Galveston, Texas. Jack Johnson began his boxing career in 1897, he quickly became an accomplished and feared fighter. In 1908, he became the first African-American Heavyweight Champion of the World when he defeated Tommy Burns in the fourteenth round in Sydney, Australia.

During his career, Johnson received a great deal of bad publicity due to his two marriages, both to Caucasian women. Interracial marriages were prohibited in most of the United States during the time. In 1912, he was convicted of violating the "Mann Act" when he transported his Caucasian wife across state lines, he was then sentenced to a year in prison.

Johnson feared for his personal safety, he escaped while he was out on appeal. He fled to Europe with his wife and remained a fugitive for seven years. In 1920, he decided to return back to the United States and serve his sentence.

Invention: While Johnson was in prison, he spent most of his time in the workshop created projects for himself, he frequently built wooden devices by hand.

He needed a special tool to help tighten and loosen some of the gadgets he was working on. In order to make his task easier, he decided to design and create the tool he needed to allow him to complete his project.

In 1922, Johnson invented the Wrench. His device had a gripping action that was superior to other tools on the market at the time, it could also be conveniently taken apart for cleaning or repair. Johnson is also credited with coining the term "Wrench."

Henry Brown

Inventions:

In 1886, Henry Brown invented the improvement to the Strongbox, known today as the Safe.

Henry Brown

Background: Henry Brown's exact birthdate and birthplace are unknown. There is not much known about his personal life or background.

Prior to Brown's invention, people often kept their valuables and documents in simple wooden box in their homes or at a local bank. These boxes provided no deterrent against burglars or bank staff with prying eyes who had access to read important documents without permission. Brown decided to create a box that was more secure.

Invention: In 1886, he invented the improved strongbox. This device was a lockable fireproof box that was divided into different compartments on the inside, it also featured a forged-metal steel container that was almost impenetrable.

Brown's invention provided security and piece of mind for anyone who needed to secure items such as gold, money, jewelry, precious documents and other valuables.

His revolutionary invention has evolved into the world's most trusted device to protect valuables. World government's, banks and people all benefit today from Brown's invention.

A larger scale version of his invention is the vault. Unlike a safe which is typically moveable, vaults are integral to the building they are located in. A vault is a secure room or a series of rooms.

Brown's ingenuity created an immense influence on the world with his vision of creating a secure environment for valuables. It lead to facilities like the United States Bullion Depository, also known as Fort Knox. Their vault is used to store a large portion of United States official gold reserves.

David Crosthwait

Inventions:

David Crosthwait has 119 patents to his name, which include 39 in the United States and 80 internationally. All of his inventions are related to heating, cooling and temperature regulating technology. He designed the HVAC (Heating Ventilation Air Conditioning) system. He also invented central air conditioning. Crosthwait revolutionized the heating and cooling industry and he was inducted into the National Inventors Hall of Fame in 2014.

David Crosthwait

(1898 - 1976)

Background: David Crosthwait was born on May 27, 1898 in Nashville, Tennessee. As a young man, Crosthwait trained to become an engineer. When he graduated from high school in Kansas City, he received a full academic scholarship to Purdue University in Indiana. In 1913, he graduated at the top of his class from Purdue and received a Bachelors Degree in Mechanical Engineering.

Crosthwait began his career working for the C.A. Dunham Company. His responsibilities were to designed and installed heating systems, he was also in charge diagnosing heating systems problems when they weren't working properly.

While at Dunham, he conducted research in several areas, including heat transfer and steam transport. His work led to many advances in HVAC devices and technology, he became very well known for his innovative solutions to heating and ventilation problems.

Invention: Crosthwait has 119 patents relating to the design, installation, testing, service of HVAC power plants, heating and ventilating systems. He pioneered most of the heating, cooling and temperature regulating technology that exist today, he also invented central air conditioning.

He was commissioned to design the heating and cooling system for Rockefeller Center and Radio City Music Hall in New York City. Due to his extraordinary work, he won a medal from the National Technological Association.

Crosthwait was the first African-American honored by the American Society of Heating, Refrigeration and Air Conditioning Engineers in 1971.

George T. Sampson

Inventions:

In 1892, George T. Sampson invented the improved Clothes Dryer. He also invented a Sled Propeller in 1885, which is the predecessor to the Snow Mobile.

George T. Sampson

(1861 - 1902)

Background: George T. Sampson was born on July 24, 1861 in Palmyra, New York. As a young man, he served several years in the United Sates Armed Forces. Once he was discharged, he developed a talent in mechanics.

Prior to his invention, the earliest versions of clothes dryers were designed in Europe in the late 18th century. The dryers were heated under an open fire, this method resulted in clothes smelling like smoke or burning altogether many times.

In the United States, the traditional way of drying clothes was using clotheslines. Clothing was hung along a rope line outdoors and attached with clothespins, the wind would eventually dry the wet clothes over a coarse of time. Sampson wanted to design an apparatus that produced a safe heat source when drying clothes.

Invention: In 1892, he invented the Ventilator Dryer. This device utilized heated air that was drawn from a stove and blown through clothing that was tumbled around in a circle. The hot air evaporated the water in the damp fabrics and accelerated the drying process.

Electric clothes dryers did not appear until 1915, the Hamilton Manufacturing Company produced the first fully automatic dryer in 1938.

Sampson's innovation paved the way paved the way for modern residential and commercial clothes dryer designs. Today 85% of all homes in the United States are equipped with a clothes dryer.

In 1885, Sampson also invented the Sled Propeller. This machine is the predecessor to the modern day snow mobile.

Dr. Lloyd Augustus Hall

Inventions:

Dr. Lloyd Augustus Hall was a Chemist who contributed to the Science of Food Preservation. In 1932, he invented a new method of Preserving Food. He has a total of 59 patents in the United States and several patents in other countries around the world. Dr. Hall was inducted into the National Inventors Hall of Fame in 2004.

Dr. Lloyd Augustus Hall

(1894 - 1971)

Background: Dr. Lloyd Augustus Hall was born on June 20, 1894 in Elgin, Illinois. Growing up, he was an honor student at the top of his class in school. He attended Northwestern University earning a Bachelors Degree in Pharmaceutical Chemistry in 1916.

In 1925, Dr. Hall was a Sr. Chemist at Griffith Laboratories. He conducted research on the chemical preservation of meat, he also devoted his time effort to food science and curing meats. Dr. Hall invented a number of ways to better preserve food. Many food preservatives used today were pioneered from his methods.

Prior to Dr. Hall's research, food preservation was a matter of chance, the most the common way of preserving food was done with salts. This method was unsatisfactory, it was difficult to keep food from spoiling and having a bitter taste.

Invention: In 1932, Hall discovered a way to use a combination of salt with tiny crystals of sodium nitrate and nitrite that suppressed the nitrogen that causes food to spoil. This was a groundbreaking discovery that forever changed the food curing process. During his career Hall had 59 U.S. patents to his name.

Dr. Hall also discovered that some spices exposed food to microbes and accelerated the process of spoiling. He then created a system to sterilize spices by using ethylene gas in a vacuum chamber that was later adapted by the Food, Drug, and Cosmetic Industries.

Dr. Hall was a pioneer in the field of Food Chemistry, he introduced new methods related to curing meats, seasonings, emulsions, bakery products, antioxidants, protein hydrolysates, and many other products that keep our food fresh.

He was also awarded several honors during his lifetime, including honorary degrees from Virginia State University, Tuskegee Institute and Howard University.

Joseph Winters

Inventions:

In 1878, Joseph Winters invented the folding Fire Escape Ladder that attaches to fire engines. In 1882, he also invented the improved Fire Escape Ladder that connects to buildings.

Joseph Winters

(1816 - 1916)

Background: Joseph R. Winters was born on August 29, 1816 in Leesburg, Virginia to a Shawnee Native-American mother and an African-American father. Winters and his family moved to Chambersburg, Pennsylvania in 1830. He was an abolitionist and active in the Underground Railroad, helping hundreds of enslaved people escape to their freedom. Winter was also close friends with fellow abolitionist Frederick Douglass.

While living in Chambersburg, Winters witnessed a huge fire destroy a downtown building. When firefighters arrived on the scene, he noticed they had to take ladders off of their wagons, climb through windows and rescue people while trying to contain the fire. Winters envisioned that firefighters should have access to ladders that could rise up directly from the wagon itself. This method would save time and make it easier to rescue people who were in danger.

Invention: In 1878, Winters invented an apparatus that included a metal frame folding ladder with parallel steps that attached onto fire wagons. This device was adopted and implemented by the Chambersburg Fire Department, they mounted his ladder on all of their horse-drawn wagons. Winters received much praise from firefighters for his invention.

During the late 19th century, many buildings were being constructed taller in U.S. cities, streets were also becoming more narrow. This new change made it difficult for firefighters to reach high floors in taller buildings.

In 1882, Winters invented the improved Fire Escape Ladder. This apparatus was designed to connect directly to the front or side of buildings. In the event of a fire or another type of emergency, everyone could safely evaluate the building using this outside ladder the climb down out of harms way and escape.

Bessie Blount Griffin

Inventions:

Bessie Blount Griffin was an Inventor, Physical Therapist and a Forensic Scientist. In 1951, she invented the Feeding Tube while working with injured World War II veterans. She also invented the Portable Receptacle Support and the Disposable Emesis Basin (the kidney shaped basins used in hospitals for medical waste).

Bessie Blount Griffin

(1914 - 2009)

Background: Bessie Blount Griffin was born on November 24, 1914 in Hickory, Virginia. Griffin received nursing training at Kennedy Memorial Hospital in New Jersey. After receiving her Nursing Degree, she attended Montclair State University.

During World War II, many volunteers were asked to assist with the war effort. Griffin already had previous training and experience working with injured veterans. She volunteered with the Gray Ladies, an organization run by the Red Cross.

Many of the veterans she treated were severely injured, some of the men she assisted lost the use of their arms or legs. While helping these men recover, Griffin decided to design an apparatus to allow the men who lost their arms to be able to independently feed themselves.

Invention: In 1951, she invented an Electronic Feeding Tube. This device allowed the men to receive a mouthful of food at a time, it was controlled by the person biting down on the tube itself. The American Veterans Administration did not accept her invention. Griffin felt strongly that injured people could benefit from her device, so she sold it to the French Government.

Griffin also invented another device for individuals with arm injuries called the Portable Receptacle Support. This apparatus was designed to hang around a person's neck. Her device allowed someone to hold items closer to their face, it was also equipped with an attachment that supported a cup or bowl. This invention was patented in the United States in 1951.

Another invention Griffin designed was the Disposable Emesis Basin, she envisioned this device could be very useful for all hospitals. Once again, the American Veterans Administration did not accept her invention, so she sold it to Belgium.

Years later, Griffin moved to Virginia to pursue a new career in law enforcement. In 1969, she worked as a Forensic Scientist at the Norfolk Police Department, she was also a chief document examiner at the Portsmouth Police Department.

Andrew Beard

Inventions:

In 1897, Andrew Beard invented the Automatic Coupler for Railroad Cars. In 1889, he also invented the Rotary Steam Engine. Beard held several other patents for farming tools and he was inducted into the National Inventors Hall of Fame in 2006.

Andrew Beard

(1849 - 1921)

Background: Andrew Beard's exact birthdate is unknown, he was born in Alabama in 1849. Beard was a slave for the first fifteen years of his life. Once he was emancipated, he became a farmer in Birmingham.

Invention: While working as a farmer, Beard was interested in the mechanics of farm equipment and the many tools he used. In 1880, he invented the Double Plow, he also invented a second type of plow in 1887. He sold the patent rights for both inventions and earned the sum of $10,000. He then used his earnings and began investing in real estate.

In 1888, Beard started a successful real estate business. Once he sold some of his properties, he earned additional $30,000. Following all of his success in real estate, Beard realized he still had a passion for inventing. He began designing different types of engines parts. In 1889, he invented the Rotary Steam Engine.

During the late 19th century, the emergence of the railroad industry had a rapid expansion throughout the United States. Beard noticed an alarming number of railroad workers had suffered serious injuries to their arms and legs during the process of coupling railroad cars. Beard himself also suffered a serious injury while coupling two railroad cars together, resulting in him losing a leg.

Car coupling was an extremely dangerous process, it involved split second timing when someone attempted to drop a metal pin in place during the precise moment two railroad cars were pulled together. Many men lost their lives or limbs attempting this task.

Beard had an idea of automating the coupling process, he wanted to make this dangerous task much safer. In 1899, he invented the Automatic Coupler for railroad cars, also known as the "Jenny Coupler." This device allowed railroads cars to automatically lock into place when they slowly bump into each other. In 1900, Beard sold the patent rights for the automatic coupler for $50,000.

Mary Beatrice Davidson Kenner

Inventions:

In 1956, Mary Beatrice Davidson Kenner invented the Sanitary Belt. She also held several other patents including a carrier attachment for an invalid walker.

Mary Beatrice Davidson Kenner

(1912 - 2006)

Background: Mary Beatrice Davidson Kenner was born on May 12, 1912 in Monroe, North Carolina. In her early years, Kenner had the spirit of ingenuity passed down from her father, he relentlessly encouraged her to explore her creativity. Kenner developed a passion for discovering and inventing new things.

Invention: In 1959, Kenner invented the Sanitary Belt. This device was a feminine hygiene product that allowed women a better way to manage their menstrual cycle. This device featured an easy to use adjustable elastic belt that was designed for women to wear that held their sanitary napkin in place (before the days of self-adhesive napkins).

Prior the her invention, women often used a variety of homemade pads that were crafted from various fabrics or other absorbent materials, these pads were secured with safety pins or clips. During the 1960s, sanitary belts were not only more practical, they were also more convenient and secure for women.

In 1959, Kenner also invented an improved version of the Sanitary Belt, this improvement featured a moisture proof napkin pocket.

Kenner's groundbreaking invention transformed feminine hygiene products. Many companies expressed interest in purchasing the patent rights for her inventions, however once they discovered she was an African-American woman, they retracted their interest.

Kenner was not interested in financial gain from her efforts, she was more concerned with making life easier for people rather than fame or fortune. Kenner also patented several other household and personal items including a carrier attachment for an invalid walker in 1959.

Charles Brooks

Inventions:

In 1896, Charles Brooks invented the improved Self Propelled Street Sweeper.

Charles Brooks

Background: Charles Brooks exact birthdate and birthplace are unknown, there is not much known about his early personal life. He was living in Newark, New Jersey when he designed and patented his famous invention.

During the end of the 19th century, many city streets in the United States were in deplorable condition. Horse-drawn carriages were the main source of transportation. Many of the horses left behind piles of waste along with litter that was discarded by pedestrians, if a celebration or parade occurred, the cleanup could take weeks.

Prior to his invention, street sweeping was a very manual and labor intense process. Teams of city workers were frequently deployed to pick up debris by hand and manually sweep using commercial brooms and shovels. There was no automated process in place at the time.

Brooks noticed the regular way of cleaning streets was extremely daunting and not very cost-effective. He decided to improve the original street sweeper design and create an apparatus that would allow street cleanup to be much faster. This machine would also ease the burden of city workers and cut their workload in half.

Invention: In 1896, Brooks invented the improved Self Propelled Street Sweeper. This machine included controlled revolving brushes that were attached to the front and the side.

These revolving brushes could also interchange with a flat scraper for the removal of snow and ice during winter months.

Brooks continued to patent improvements to his street sweeper design, including a receptacle for storing the collected garbage and a wheel located inside for controlling the external rotating brushes. City workers praised Brooks for his invention, it made their job much easier to maintain the debris on city streets. Due to his innovation, the modern day street sweepers which are used by city sanitation departments are capable of removing tons of debris each day.

Sarah Boone

Inventions:

Sarah Boone is the second African-American woman to receive a U.S. Patent. In 1892, she invented the improved Ironing Board.

Sarah Boone

(1832 – 1904)

Background: Sarah Boone was born Sarah Marshall in Mississippi in 1832, her exact birthdate is unknown. At the age of fifteen she married a man named James Boone, the couple had eight children.

Boone and her family decided to leave Mississippi before the outbreak of the Civil War, they moved to New Haven, Connecticut where she began a successful career as a professional seamstress.

During the mid 1800's, most people ironed their clothes using a wooden board rested between a pair of chairs or across a table. The ironing was done with an iron that was preheated on a kitchen stove.

In Boone's line of business, she created custom clothing for women such as dresses, blouses and evening gowns. She needed a reliable and convenient device to iron her clothing on while working in her store.

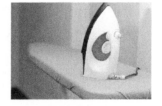

Invention: In 1892, Boone was awarded the patent for her invention of the improved ironing board. The popularity of her invention grew very quickly due to its sleek and sophisticated design.

Her ironing board was made of a narrow wooden board that featured collapsible legs and a padded cover, it was designed to be folded and put away in a closet or another small confined area.

Her ironing board improved the quality of ironing long sleeves and other parts of men and women's garments. Boone was the second African-American woman that was awarded a U.S. Patent.

Norbert Rillieux

Inventions:

Norbert Rillieux revolutionized the sugar industry. In 1843, he invented a refining process that was responsible for transforming sugar into a household item. Rillieux was inducted into the National Inventors Hall of Fame in 2004.

Norbert Rillieux

(1806 - 1894)

Background: Norbert Rillieux was born on March 17, 1806 in New Orleans, Louisiana. He was was born a free man although his mother was a slave. His father was a wealthy French engineer who was involved in the cotton industry. In 1830, his father sent him to Paris, France to earn an education at L'Ecole Centrale, where he studied Evaporating Engineering. Rillieux returned back home to New Orleans in 1833.

When Rillieux returned back to the United States, he discovered sugarcane had become the dominant crop within Louisiana. He viewed the methods of refining it into sugar as extremely dangerous and crude. He spoke out against the harsh treatment of slaves, who had to endure the treacherous back-breaking labor.

Prior to Rillieux's famous invention, the sugar refining process (known as the Jamaica Train) threatened the safety of the many slaves. They were forced to transport boiling hot cane juice from one kettle to another in order to produce sugar, there was a possibility they could suffer severe burns in the process. Along with the process being extremely dangerous, it was also costly considering the amount of fuel needed to heat the various kettles.

Invention: In 1843, Rillieux invented a Multiple Effect Evaporator. This apparatus heated the sugarcane juice in a partial vacuum, reducing its boiling point while also allowing a much greater fuel efficiency. The sugar crystals then came out white instead of black or brown. Rillieux's invention took much of the labor out of the refining process and was solely responsible for transforming sugar into a household item.

Sugar manufacturers in Cuba, Mexico, France and Egypt all adopted Rillieux's evaporator. His invention revolutionized the refining industry and it still exist today for sugar production as well as condensed milk, soap, glue and many other products.

Dr. Mark Dean

Inventions:

Dr. Dean was instrumental in the invention of the Personal Computer. He holds three of IBM's original nine Personal Computer patents and currently holds more than 20 total patents. Dr. Dean was also inducted into the National Inventors Hall of Fame in 1997.

Dr. Mark Dean

(1957–)

Background: Dr. Mark Dean was born on March 2, 1957 in Jefferson City, Tennessee. Dr. Dean holds a Bachelors Degree in Electrical Engineering from the University of Tennessee, a Master's Degree in Electrical Engineering from Florida Atlantic University and a Ph.D in Electrical Engineering from Stanford University. He began his career working at IBM as a Computer Scientist.

Invention: Dr. Dean was one of the original inventors of the IBM personal computer as well as the color PC monitor. He is also responsible for creating the technology that allows devices such as keyboards, mice, and printers to communicate with each other while being plugged into a computer.

In 1999, he managed the team that created the world's first Gigahertz Processor Chip, a revolutionary piece of technology that is able to complete a billion calculations per second. He holds three of the company's original nine personal computer patents and currently holds more than 20 patents associated with his name.

In 1995, Dr. Dean was the first African-American to become an IBM Fellow, which is the highest level of technical excellence at the company.

In 1997, he was inducted into the National Inventors Hall of Fame. In 2004, Dr. Dean was also selected as one of the 50 most important African-Americans in Research Science.

Dr. Dean's inventions have changed the world, his innovation has allowed billions people to use personal computers in their homes, offices and schools each day worldwide.

Michael A. Carson

U.S. Patent Information

A list of U.S Patent Information for all of the inventors mentioned. The list is complete with publication numbers, publication dates and a brief description of their invention.

George Washington Carver

U.S Patent US1522176A 01/26/1925 Improvements in Cosmetics

U.S Patent US1632365A 06/14/1927 Process of Producing Paints

Lewis Latimer

U.S Patent US147363A 02/10/1874 Water Closet for Railroad-Cars

U.S Patent US247097A 09/13/1881 Electric Lamp

U.S. Patent US252386A 01/17/1882 Process of Manufacturing Carbons

U.S. Patent US255212A 03/21/1882 Supporter for Electric Lamps

U.S. Patent US334078A 01/12/1886 Apparatus for Cooling

U.S. Patent US557076A 03/24/1896 Locking Rack for Hats and Coats

U.S. Patent US968787A 08/30/1910 Lamp Fixture

Garrett Morgan

U.S. Patent US1113675A 10/20/1914 Breathing Device (Gas Mask)

U.S. Patent US1475024A 11/20/1923 Traffic Signal

U.S. Patent US2762382A 09/11/1956 Comb for Straightening Hair

Dr. Charles Richard Drew

U.S. Patent US2301710A 11/10/1942 Apparatus for Preserving Blood

U.S. Patent US2389355A 11/20/1945 Surgical Needle

U.S. Patent US2397257A 03/26/1946 Surgical Suction Apparatus

Otis Boykin

U.S. Patent US2634352A 04/07/1953 Electrical Resistor

U.S. Patent US2758267A 08/07/1956 Silver Conductors

U.S. Patent US2891227A 06/15/1959 Wire Type Precision Resistor

U.S. Patent US3191108A 06/22/1965 Electrical Capacitor

U.S. Patent US2972726A 02/21/1961 Electrical Resistor

U.S. Patent US3304199A 02/14/1967 Electrical Resistance Element

U.S. Patent US3329526A 07/04/1967 Electrical Resistance Element

U.S. Patent US3348971A 10/24/1967 Method Making Film Capacitor

U.S. Patent US3394290A 07/23/1968 Thin Film Capacitor

U.S. Patent US4267074A 05/12/1981 Self Supporting Resistor

Elijah McCoy

U.S. Patent	US783382A	02/21/1905	Journal Lubricator
U.S. Patent	US856084A	06/04/1907	Scaffold Support
U.S. Patent	US926588A	06/29/1909	Steam Cannon Apparatus
U.S. Patent	US947738A	01/25/1910	Buggy Top Support
U.S. Patent	US997400A	07/11/1911	Lubricator
U.S. Patent	US1021255A	03/26/1912	Gage
U.S. Patent	US1031948A	07/09/1912	Lubricator
U.S. Patent	US1101868A	09/24/1912	Valve and Plug
U.S. Patent	US1097134A	05/19/1914	Locomotive Lubricator
U.S. Patent	US1109775A	09/08/1914	Lubricator
U.S. Patent	US1136689A	04/20/1915	Locomotive Lubricator
U.S. Patent	US1192083A	07/25/1916	Lubricator
U.S. Patent	US1338385A	04/27/1920	Air brake-pump Lubricator
U.S. Patent	US1499468A	07/01/1924	Lubricator
U.S. Patent	US1558266A	10/20/1925	Lubricator
U.S. Patent	US1574983A	03/02/1926	Lubricator

Madam C.J. Walker

U.S Patent US1716173A 06/04/1929 Scalp Protector

Alexander Miles

U.S. Patent US371207A 10/11/1887 Elevator

Jan Ernst Matzeliger

U.S. Patent US274207A 03/20/1883 Automatic Method for
    Lasting Shoes

U.S. Patent US421954A 02/25/1890 Nailing Machine

U.S. Patent US423937A 03/25/1890 Tack Separating and Distributing

U.S. Patent US415726A 11/26/1899 Mechanism for Distributing Tacks

Granville T. Wood

U.S. Patent	US639692A	09/27/1898	Amusement Apparatus
U.S. Patent	US656760A	05/25/1900	Incubator
U.S. Patent	US662049A	11/20/1900	Automatic Circuit Breaker
U.S. Patent	US667110A	01/29/1901	Electric Railway
U.S. Patent	US678086A	07/09/1901	Electric Railway
U.S. Patent	US681768A	09/03/1901	Regulate Electrical Devices
U.S. Patent	US690810A	01/07/1902	Apparatus for Electric Motors
U.S. Patent	US695988A	03/25/1902	Electric Railway
U.S. Patent	US697928A	04/15/1902	Motor Controlling Apparatus
U.S. Patent	US697767A	04/15/1902	System of Electrical Control
U.S. Patent	US701981A	06/10/1902	Automatic Air Brake
U.S. Patent	US718183A	01/13/1903	Electric Railway System
U.S. Patent	US729481A	05/26/1903	Electric Railway
U.S. Patent	US755825A	03/29/1904	Railroad Brake Apparatus
U.S. Patent	US762792A	06/14/1904	Electric Railroad Apparatus
U.S. Patent	US795243A	07/18/1905	Railroad Brake Apparatus
U.S. Patent	US833193A	10/16/1906	Safety Apparatus for Railroads
U.S. Patent	US837022A	11/27/1906	Safety Apparatus for Railroads
U.S. Patent	US867180A	09/24/1907	Vehicle Controlling Apparatus

George Franklin Grant

U.S. Patent   US638920A   12/12/1899   Golf Tee

Benjamin Banneker

Invented first Clock in the United States, also surveyed and designed the plans for the layout of Washington D.C.

Gerald Lawson

Invented the World's first Video Gaming System using interchangeable cartridges.

Benjamin F. Thornton

U.S. Patent   US1831331A 11/10/1931 Apparatus for automatically Recording Telephone Messages

Dr. Patricia Bath

U.S. Patent   US4744360A 05/17/1988 Apparatus for Removing Cataract

Dr. Henry T. Sampson

U.S. Patent   US3591860A 07/06/1971 Gamma-Electric Cell

Sarah E. Goode

First African-American woman to receive a U.S. patent.

U.S. Patent   US322177A   07/14/1885 Cabinet Bed

George Murray

U.S. Patent	US517961A	04/10/1894	Cultivator and Marker
U.S. Patent	US520888A	06/05/1894	Cotton Chopper
U.S. Patent	US520889A	06/05/1894	Fertilizer Distributer
U.S. Patent	US520890A	06/05/1894	Planter
U.S. Patent	US520891A	06/05/1894	Cotton Seed Planter
U.S. Patent	US641030A	01/09/1900	Road Breaker and Scraper
U.S. Patent	US642555A	01/30/1900	Potato Digging Machinery
U.S. Patent	US644032A	02/20/1900	Grain Drill

Thomas Elkins

U.S. Patent	US100020A	02/22/1870	Improvement Dining Table
U.S. Patent	US122518A	01/09/1872	Improvement Commode
U.S. Patent	US221222A	11/04/1879	Improvement Refrigerator

Marie Van Brittan Brown

U.S. Patent	US3482037A	12/02/1969	Home Security System Utilizing Television Surveillance

Richard Spikes

U.S. Patent	US850070A	01/12/1907	Beer Tapper
U.S. Patent	US928813A	07/20/1908	Beer Tapper
U.S. Patent	US871073A	11/12/1908	Beer Tapper
U.S. Patent	US972277A	10/11/1910	Billiard Cue Rack
U.S. Patent	US1362197A	12/14/1920	Trolley-Pole Arrester
U.S. Patent	US1441388A	09/21/1921	Brake Testing Machine
U.S. Patent	US1461988A	07/17/1923	Pantograph
U.S. Patent	US1590557A	02/24/1925	Milk Bottle Opener and Cover
U.S. Patent	US18889814A	12/06/1932	Automatic Gear Shift
U.S. Patent	US1936996A	11/28/1933	Transmission and Shifting
U.S. Patent	US2517936A	08/20/1950	Horizontal Swing Barber Chair
U.S. Patent	US3015522A	01/02/1962	Automatic Safety Brake

Philip Downing

U.S. Patent	US430118A	06/17/1890	Street Railway Switch
U.S. Patent	US462093A	10/27/1891	Letter Box (Street Mailbox)

Daniel Hale Williams

Performed the first Successful Open Heart Surgery Procedure in the United States.

George Crum

Invented Potato Chips.

John Albert Burr

U.S. Patent	US624749A	05/09/1899	Lawn Mower

Frederick Jones

U.S. Patent	US2376968A	05/29/1945	Two-Cycle Gas Engine
U.S. Patent	US2475841A	07/12/1949	Air Conditioning Unit
U.S. Patent	US2475842A	07/12/1949	Starter Generator
U.S. Patent	US2504841A	04/18/1950	Rotary Compressor
U.S. Patent	US2926005A	02/23/1960	Thermostat Control
US. Patent	US2850001A	09/14/1955	Control Device for Engine

Thomas Jennings

First African-American man to receive a U.S. patent.

The Patent Act of 1836 resulted in patents receiving numbers listed chronologically from the time they had been first issued, assigning patent number 3,306x to Jennings invention, with the x indicating that the patent had been registered before 1836.

Details of Jennings patent were lost in a fire at the U.S. Patent Office in 1836, most patent records were stored there including Jennings application and any associated materials supporting it. The application and specific information with Jennings description of his invention remain uncertain.

U.S Patent	3,306x	03/03/1821	Dry Cleaning

Henry Blair

Second African-American man to receive a U.S. patent.

U.S. Patent	X8447	10/14/1834	Seed Planter
U.S. Patent	US15A	08/31/1836	Cotton Planter

William Purvis

U.S. Patent	US419065A	01/07/1890	Fountain Pen
U.S. Patent	US256856A	04/25/1882	Bag Fastener
U.S. Patent	US519349A	05/08/1894	Paper Bag Machine

Jack Johnson

U.S. Patent	US1413121A	04/18/1922	Wrench

Henry Brown

U.S. Patent	US352036A	11/02/1886	Strongbox (Safe)

David Crosthwait

U.S. Patent	US1353457A	09/21/1920	Return Water to Boilers
U.S. Patent	US1473670A	11/23/1923	Forming Radiator
U.S. Patent	US1694164A	12/04/1928	Setting Thermostat
U.S. Patent	US1986391A	05/05/1929	Vacuum Heating System
U.S. Patent	US1755430A	04/22/1930	Differential Vacuum Pump
U.S. Patent	US1946524A	05/15/1931	Vacuum Pump
U.S. Patent	US1871044A	08/09/1932	Automatic Discharge Valve
U.S. Patent	US1874911A	08/30/1932	Temperature Indicator
U.S Patent	US1977303A	10/16/1934	Steam Heating System
U.S. Patent	US1977304A	11/16/1934	Steam Heating Apparatus
U.S. Patent	US2096226A	04/17/1935	Exhausting Apparatus
U.S. Patent	US2102197A	12/14/1937	One Pipe Heating System
U.S. Patent	US2114139A	04/12/1938	Regulating Radiator Valve
U.S. Patent	US2185500A	01/02/1940	Heat Balancer
U.S. Patent	US2275132A	03/03/1942	Discharge Valve
U.S. Patent	US2346560A	04/11/1944	Window Thermostat
U.S. Patent	US2362977A	11/21/1944	Indicator System
U.S. Patent	US2431790A	12/02/1947	Temperature Apparatus
U.S. Patent	US3478625A	11/18/1969	Tool for Adjusting Valves

George T. Sampson

U.S. Patent	US476416A	06/07/1892	Clothes Dryer
U.S. Patent	US312388A	02/17/1885	Sled Propeller

Dr. Lloyd Augustus Hall

U.S. Patent	US1995121A	06/16/1934	Stabilized Solid Seasoning
U.S. Patent	US2107697A	05/29/1936	Sterilizing Food
U.S. Patent	US2097405A	10/26/1937	Bleached Pepper Products
U.S. Patent	US2145417A	01/31/1939	Stabilized Nitrite Salt
U.S. Patent	US2171428A	08/29/1939	Composition of Matter
U.S. Patent	US2189949A	02/13/1940	Sterilizing Colloid Material
U.S. Patent	US2189948A	02/13/1940	Sterilizing of Pancreatin
U.S. Patent	US2464200A	02/24/1945	Stable Dry Composition
U.S. Patent	US2477742A	08/02/1949	Gelatin Base Food Coating
U.S. Patent	US2500543A	03/14/1950	Antioxidant
U.S. Patent	US2571867A	07/21/1950	Spice Extraction Product
U.S. Patent	US2553533A	05/15/1951	Curing Process for Bacon
U.S. Patent	US2571948A	10/16/1951	Spice Extraction Method
U.S. Patent	US2770551A	11/13/1956	Meat Curing Composition
U.S. Patent	US2938766A	05/31/1960	Sterilizing Hospital Supplies

Joseph Winters

U.S. Patent	US203517A	05/07/1878	Improve Fire Escape Ladder
U.S. Patent	US214224A	04/08/1979	Improve Fire Escape Ladder
U.S. Patent	US167966A	01/11/1875	Improvement Farm Fences

Bessie Blount Griffin

U.S. Patent	US2550554A	04/24/1951	Portable Receptacle Support

Andrew Beard

U.S Patent	US240642A	09/04/1880	Double Plow
U.S Patent	US462614A	11/03/1891	Rotary Engine
U.S Patent	US478271A	07/05/1892	Rotary Engine
U.S Patent	US624901A	05/16/1899	Car-Coupling
U.S Patent	US675346A	05/28/1901	Automatic Car Coupling
U.S Patent	US807430A	12/19/1905	Automatic Car Coupler

Mary Beatrice Davidson Kenner

U.S Patent	US2745406A	05/15/1956	Sanitary Belt
U.S Patent	US2881761A	04/14/1959	Sanitary Belt
U.S Patent	US3957071A	05/18/1976	Attachment Invalid Walker

Charles Brooks

U.S Patent	US558719A	04/21/1896	Street Sweeper
U.S Patent	US560154A	05/12/1896	Street Sweeper Bag
U.S Patent	US507672A	10/31/1883	Hole Puncher

Sarah Boone

U.S. Patent	US473653A	04/26/1892	Ironing Board

Norbert Rillieux

U.S. Patent	US3237A	08/26/1843	Improvement in Sugar
U.S. Patent	US4879A	12/10/1846	Improvement in Sugar

Dr. Mark Dean

U.S. Patent   US4437092A   03/13/1984   Color Video Display System
Having Programmable
Border Color

U.S. Patent   US4442428A   04/10/1984   Composite Video Color
Signal Generation from
Digital Color Signals

U.S. Patent   US4575826A   03/11/1986   Refresh Generator System
for a Dynamic Memory

U.S. Patent   US4598356A   07/01/1986   Data Processing System
Including a Main Processor
and a co-processor and co-
processor Error Handling
Logic

Michael A. Carson

WORK CITED

European Patent Office.

National Inventors Hall of Fame.

Natural Museum of African-American History and Culture.

New York Public Library.

United States Censes Records.

United States Patent and Trade Office.

Michael A. Carson

ACKNOWLEDGEMENTS

As always, I have to begin by giving thanks to God, for guiding my life and giving my family and I his infinite blessings.

To my lovely wife Shenika and our son Matthew.

To my parents Mary and Sam, who gave me life and taught me how to love God and Family.

To my sister and brother-in-law Sandra and Arthur. To my brother and sister-in-law Sanford and Bridget. Thank you for your love and support.

To my nieces and nephews, Serena, Stephanie, Shayla, Jayda, Keiana, Darius, Darin and Austin.

To the entire Carson, Street, Hall and Bolden families. Much love to all of you.

Michael A. Carson

ABOUT THE AUTHOR

Michael A. Carson is a husband and father. He was born and raised in Queens, New York. He has a Bachelors Degree in Psychology from Virginia State University. He now resides with his family in Atlanta, Georgia working as a Government Analyst.

What began as a conversation teaching his son about African-American inventors, continued as a passion for Michael. He wanted to educate the next generation about the many contributions African-American inventors have made in our society.

Michael and his wife Shenika co-founded Double Infinity Publishing. Their goal is to publish high quality literature that represents historical facts as well as provide a voice and platform for educating readers.

Michael A. Carson

Michael A. Carson

Michael A. Carson

Michael A. Carson

Made in the USA
Monee, IL
19 September 2022

14272197R00080